Cool Careers in
ENVIRONMENTAL SCIENCES

Sally Ride
Science

CONTENTS

Mary

Camille

Tyrone

INTRODUCTION 4

ASTRONAUT
Mary Cleave 6

CLIMATE CHANGE BIOLOGIST
Camille Parmesan 8

DEVELOPMENTAL BIOLOGIST
Tyrone Hayes 10

ENERGY ENGINEER
Surya Santoso 12

ENVIRONMENTAL FILM PRODUCER
Chris Palmer 14

ENVIRONMENTAL LAWYER
Margaret Caldwell 16

Surya

Chris

Margaret

Tommy

Weslynne

Sylvia

ENVIRONMENTAL SCIENCE TEACHER
Tommy Hayes 18

INDUSTRIAL ECOLOGIST
Weslynne Ashton 20

OCEANOGRAPHER
Sylvia Earle 22

Rodolfo

TROPICAL ECOLOGIST
Rodolfo Dirzo 24

WATER ENGINEER
Susan Murcott 26

Susan

WILDLIFE OFFICER
Windi Padia 28

Windi

ABOUT ME 30

CAREERS 4 U! 32

GLOSSARY and INDEX 34

ANSWER KEY 36

What Do You Want to Be?

Is working in environmental sciences one of your goals?

The good news is that there are many different paths leading there. The people who work in environmental sciences come from many different backgrounds and include ecologists, biologists, geologists, oceanographers, climatologists, environmental writers, teachers, and more.

It's never too soon to think about what you want to be. You probably have lots of things that you like to do—maybe you like doing experiments or helping others. Or maybe you like working with numbers or writing stories.

SALLY RIDE
First American Woman in Space

The women and men you're about to meet found their careers by doing what they love. As you read this book and do the activities, think about what you like doing. Then follow your interests, and see where they take you. You just might find your career, too.

Reach for the stars!

Sally K Ride

"To understand how Earth works, you have to understand and appreciate oceans."

Water World

Looking out the Shuttle window with her environmental engineer's eye, Mary saw the power of Earth's enormous oceans and plant life that affects us all. Today, Mary collects satellite data on microscopic ocean plants called phytoplankton. "They remove carbon dioxide, a gas that causes global warming, from the air," she says. Tiny plants, big job.

MARY CLEAVE
Sigma Space Corporation

Supersonic Environmentalist

Mary Cleave learned to fly when she was 14, but she never dreamed she'd fly in space. Instead, in college she studied botany. She later became an environmental engineer, studying plant life in lakes and oceans. But when NASA was looking for engineers to work in space, Mary jumped at the chance. "It sounded like fun," Mary says, "especially when I learned that I'd get to fly T-38 jets as part of my training."

Space Wizard

When Mary was a kid she loved *Watch Mr. Wizard*, a TV program that featured cool science experiments. Years later, as an astronaut on the Space Shuttle, Mary performed some wizardry of her own. She helped launch the *Magellan* spacecraft from the Shuttle, sending it on its way to map the surface of Venus.

The *Magellan* spacecraft is released from the Shuttle bay.

An astronaut travels into space to explore Earth and beyond. Today, with the help of satellites in space, Mary measures the amount of plant life in the oceans. Other **astronauts**

* test rockets and spacecraft.
* study the effects of low gravity on people, plants, and animals.
* repair satellites and other instruments orbiting Earth.
* conduct scientific experiments on the space station.

Mary flew on two Shuttle missions. This is the crew of STS-30.

Phyto Flight

When Mary compared satellite images of the ocean, she found that the number of phytoplankton is going down. Why? It's because the oceans are getting warmer. That's a problem because phytoplankton are producers. During photosynthesis they produce the food that starts most ocean food chains.

With a classmate, research food chains. Then create a science poster that shows who eats whom in this food chain—zooplankton, Arctic cod, phytoplankton, and ringed seal. Which way should the arrows point to show the flow of energy, or food? Why? Write a caption that explains how warming ocean temperatures might affect this food chain.

Is It 4 U?

What parts of an astronaut's job sound most exciting to you? Think about it, and then talk to a classmate about what he or she would like about the job.

- Floating weightless
- Examining Earth from space
- Conducting experiments in space
- Staying on the space station

Crunch and Chuckle

Q. What are Mary's favorite nuts?

A. Astro-nuts.

Check out your answers on page 36.

"What excites me most about my job is being in the wilderness. It's what I've loved since I could walk."

CAMILLE PARMESAN
University of Texas at Austin

Butterfly Buddies

In college, Camille Parmesan studied all kinds of animals—from honeybees to monkeys. But when Camille started studying a butterfly called Edith's checkerspot, she found her future. The 4½ years Camille spent tracking the butterfly led to a groundbreaking discovery. In response to climate change, the butterfly has disappeared from many of its habitats in Mexico and southern California. It's moving north and up the mountains to areas that are cooler places to live. Camille's research gave her the opportunity to work in her favorite lab, the outdoors. She hiked and camped from Mexico to Canada." The butterflies have a schedule that is perfect for me," Camille says. "They wake up at 10 A.M. and go to bed at 4 P.M."

White House or Wilderness?

Camille's work has launched her into the spotlight. She's been featured in newspapers across the country and appeared on TV talk shows. She's even been invited to speak at the White House.

Big Answers

"Don't be afraid of looking for answers to big questions," Camille says. That's how she's provided the first evidence that Earth's creatures are struggling to adapt to climate change. She has become an expert on the effect of climate change on plants and animals around the globe. Camille has figured out that many other species are moving north, including dragonflies, rufous hummingbirds, starfish, and red foxes.

"I eat really well while camping—we're talking lamb chops with sautéed asparagus."

A climate change biologist

A climate change biologist studies the effects of Earth's warming air, land, and ocean temperatures on plants and animals and their habitats. Camille studies the life and behavior of Edith's checkerspot butterfly. Other **climate change biologists**

✳ investigate the impact of warmer ocean waters on coral reefs.

✳ analyze how increased carbon dioxide in the air affects forests.

✳ study how polar bears are responding to living with less Arctic sea ice.

✳ measure the shifting ranges of birds or trees.

Edith's checkerspot butterflies have a pattern that's like a checkerboard.

Sights and Smells

"When I think about my career, it all comes back to my mother," Camille says. "She inspired me." Camille's mom was a geologist. On weekend field trips she made their surroundings come alive. They used a field guide to identify the sights and smells around them—from flowers to rocks to seashells. Who inspires you? Write a short essay about that person. Be sure to include why and how they inspire you.

Mini-Ecosystem

Doing fieldwork is what Camille loves most. Now it's your turn. Predict what you might find by observing a small part of your schoolyard ecosystem—under a rock, around a tree, or in the grass. Then cut a square out of the middle of a piece of cardboard, leaving a 1-inch border. Use this eco-frame to place over and focus on your area. Observe this area at different times of the day. Record your observations in a field journal. Be sure to include the date, time, and any notes.

• What living organisms are in your mini-ecosystem?
• What are the nonliving parts of it?
• In what ways do the living organisms interact with each other and their nonliving surroundings?

Summarize your observations to share with your class. How did your observations match your predictions? How did they differ?

9

TYRONE HAYES
University of California, Berkeley

From Curiosity to Career

"I've always been in love with wildlife and nature," says Tyrone Hayes. As a boy, he explored the swamps near his South Carolina home. He loved to watch the turtles, snakes, and toads. But watching tadpoles turn into frogs was his favorite thing to do. Even today, Tyrone is often knee-deep in water—such as African swamps and Midwestern ponds—looking for frogs. He turned his childhood passion into his career.

Natural and Unnatural

"I like solving puzzles," says Tyrone. One puzzle he's working on is why African reed frogs change color. While doing fieldwork in Africa, Tyrone noticed some male frogs weren't their normal solid green. Instead, they'd taken on the colorfully spotty look of female frogs. Why? Back in his California laboratory, Tyrone studied thousands of reed frogs collected in Kenya and Tanzania. He learned that as tadpoles develop into frogs, their thin skin is super-sensitive. If the frogs live in water contaminated with pesticides, chemicals pass through their skin. Tyrone showed how those chemicals can trigger a color change—another piece of the puzzle!

"What affects our amphibian friends can also affect us," says Tyrone.

Rivet-ing Results

Tyrone has learned that many environmental pollutants harm frogs. They trigger all sorts of changes including in size, shape, and behavior. He's seen frogs with extra legs and giant tadpoles that never become frogs.

A frog net and wader boots are just two of the tools Tyrone uses doing field work.

A developmental biologist

studies all the changes a living organism goes through during its life cycle, from a single cell to an adult. Tyrone studies the development of frogs and other amphibians, and how water pollution affects them. Other **developmental biologists**

Tyrone studies leopard frogs in the field and in his lab.

* study mouse embryos to better understand how mammals develop.

* investigate how stem cells become heart cells or brain cells.

* observe fruit flies to better understand how humans inherit their genes.

Frog versus Toad

Can you tell the difference between a frog and a toad? Research the characteristics of each—where they live, what their bodies are like, and what they eat. Then make a Venn diagram that compares and contrasts frogs and toads.

Is It 4 U?

Tyrone enjoys

* doing fieldwork to study frogs.
* traveling around the world to work with other scientists.
* solving science puzzles.

What do you have in common with Tyrone? Discuss with a partner what you think would make you a good biologist, and why.

U the Biologist

New species of frogs and other amphibians are being discovered all the time. Imagine you're a globe-trotting biologist conducting research in the wild. To your surprise, you come across a new amphibian. Work with a team to create an oral presentation for other biologists that

* describes what you found.
* tells how you felt about your discovery.
* names the type of ecosystem it lives in—forest, desert, wetland.
* details how you would study it to learn more about it.

Oh . . . and don't forget to name your new species!

Check out your answers on page 36.

"As an engineer, I design solutions—like getting clean energy to more people."

SURYA SANTOSO
University of Texas at Austin

Powerhouse in the Sky

Surya Santoso grabs energy out of thin air. What's the trick? No trick—it's wind power! When the wind blows, it spins the blades of giant wind turbines, producing electricity. In Surya's home state of Texas, the wind powers about a million homes. That reduces the need to generate electricity from less environmentally-friendly sources of energy—like coal. So, Texans are eager to make even more wind power. What's the catch?

On and Off

The catch is that you can't control the wind. "Wind power is variable. We can't always accurately predict it," says Surya. Variable can mean unreliable—you can't always count on the wind to supply electricity. Or can you? That's where Surya comes in. No wind? No problem! Surya is researching ways to store the extra energy made when the wind really blows. One idea is to store it as mechanical energy—just like a windup toy. That way the energy can be released when there isn't enough wind to spin the wind turbines. Wind is an excellent source of clean renewable energy. But managing it isn't always a breeze!

It All Adds Up

In sixth grade, Surya dreamed of becoming an engineer, but he struggled with math. So Surya worked harder. "I didn't get good at math until I was in high school," Surya says. That's when he started to make his dream come true.

Texas blows away the competition! It leads the U.S. in wind power.

An energy engineer designs systems that send electricity from one place to another. Surya creates ways to store power from wind turbines. Other **energy engineers**

✳ manage the power grid that sends electricity to homes and businesses.

✳ build and install devices that send out power with the correct current.

✳ design new sources of energy and new ways to use energy.

Blowing in the Wind

Woosh! There's power in wind. A 250 kilowatt (kW) wind turbine produces 350,000 kW hours of electricity per year. The average U.S. household uses about 10,655 kW hours of electricity per year. Use a calculator to figure out how many households the wind turbine can supply with power.

On the Rise

In 2007, renewable energies—wind, solar, geothermal, and biofuels—provided 8.4 percent of all electricity in the U.S. By the year 2030, the U.S. Department of Energy predicts renewable energies will increase to at least 12.5 percent. Create two circle graphs—one for 2007 and one for 2030. In each, compare the percentage of renewable energy with nonrenewable energy—oil, coal, and natural gas. Why is it important to keep increasing the renewable energy wedge of the circle graphs?

How Green Is Your School?

Talk to your teacher about forming a green team to investigate the environmental impact of your school—and where it's wasting energy and money. Check out

- the classrooms and bathrooms.
- the auditorium and main office.
- the cafeteria and library.
- the gym and playground.
- the bus and car drop-off zone.

When the team is finished, analyze your results. Then create a Going Green Action Plan. What changes can be made quickly and easily with little or no cost? What changes need long-term planning? Your goal? Lower your school's environmental impact by saving energy and recycling. Get everyone involved, and get going!

CHRIS PALMER

American University

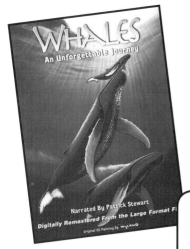

"I never dreamed I'd be an environmentalist. Who knows where you'll end up, so keep dreaming."

No Quiet on the Set

Chris Palmer has come face-to-face with Kodiak bears. He's camped with wolves and confronted sharks. It's all in a day's work! Chris produces films, TV specials, and IMAX movies about wildlife and the environment. The movie stars he works with range from dolphins and tigers to coral reefs and rain forests. His movies are shot in locations all around the planet—from high atop Mount Everest to deep in the ocean.

From Real to Reel Life

As a producer, Chris starts with just an idea. Then he hires a crew, arranges for the filming and editing, and organizes every step it takes to get the movie to the big screen. Chris started with a college degree in ocean engineering and combined it with his love for the environment—the result is movie magic. Of the dozens of films he's made, his favorite is *Whales*. "On location, I had a chance to swim with the humpback whales. Imagine. Each female is the size of six elephants. They're powerful yet there's a profound serenity about them."

Movies to Move You

Chris sees movies as a way to get out his message—our planet needs protection. "There are many ways to get involved. One is to move people to action," Chris says.

WHALES
An Unforgettable Journey
Narrated By Patrick Stewart
Digitally Remastered From the Large Format Fi
Original Oil Painting By Wyland

"Whales are still being hunted. I'll do anything to stop that."

An environmental film producer makes movies about topics that affect the environment. Chris makes movies and TV specials that bring environmental issues to the screen. Other **environmental film producers**

* make documentaries about environmental disasters such as oil spills or natural fires.

* produce films about animals for zoos, museums, and national park visitor centers.

* film educational shows about endangered wildlife.

* create ads that help wildlife organizations raise money to protect wildlife.

The Write Stuff

Film production usually starts with an idea for a script. Put yourself in a producer's chair by reviewing the following script ideas. Which one would you most like to produce? Discuss your choice with a classmate.

- A documentary investigating California's wildfires
- A TV special explaining the importance of recycling
- An IMAX movie about how global warming is harming coral reefs
- A story line about the effects of overfishing tuna in the ocean

Lights, Camera, Eco-Action!

Put yourself in the director's chair. Think of how you would bring alive the idea you chose for "The Write Stuff." Put your thoughts into a letter to the head of a studio that could fund your project. Here are some things to include in your letter.

- Who would be the subjects of your story?
- Where would you set it?
- What kind of scientist would you hire to make sure the story is accurate?
- Who would you want your film to inspire?

Is It 4 U?

Do you have a future in film? Discuss with a classmate which parts of Chris's job you would like.

- Traveling into the wilderness to film wildlife
- Seeing your work on the big screen
- Interviewing scientists to get accurate information about wildlife
- Working with computers, cameras, and editing tools to produce the finished product

MARGARET CALDWELL

Stanford University

"I love to walk on the beach. The animals I see are part of the web of life I'm working to protect."

Oceans Alive

Sea otters snack on spiny sea urchins. Packs of bottlenose dolphins whistle to each other. Rockfish cruise the seafloor. The ocean is alive, packed with 80 percent of all life on Earth. Many human activities, however, threaten marine life, such as oil drilling, overfishing, and even the noise from ships. The biggest threat of all is climate change, which is causing the world's oceans to warm. Who can protect the ocean creatures? Meet Meg Caldwell.

Waterproofing

"The ocean is my client," Meg says. And like all good lawyers, Meg is working hard to defend this giant client. Right now there are many different organizations and government groups looking after the California coast. Meg and her team are developing one set of guidelines to protect California's coastal waters and marine life—based on the latest studies by environmental scientists. Luckily, Meg is a very good translator. For example, she can explain an ecologist's research on tide pools so it makes sense to government officials. Meg stands up for her client— with one foot in science and one foot in the law.

Water Baby

Meg's dad was in the Navy, so she grew up on both the Atlantic and Pacific coasts. Her backyard was the ocean where she went tide pooling, whale watching, and body surfing. "I grew up having a deep curiosity about the oceans and enormous respect for its power," Meg says.

Meg works with a student, analyzing samples of sea water from a local beach.

An environmental lawyer

An environmental lawyer uses the law to protect the environment and wildlife. Meg protects the animals and plants that live along the coast of California. Other **environmental lawyers**

* file lawsuits against companies that pollute the land.
* advise industrial companies on how to follow recycling laws.
* work with representatives and senators to write environmental legislation.

Sea otters are classified as an endangered species.

Your Turn

Meg is a good translator. She can explain environmental studies to government officials. Try your hand at explaining something to someone else. Pick your favorite hobby such as sports, music, or art. Write about one specific part of it in detail. For example, how to serve in tennis, how to tune a guitar, or how to make a paper airplane. Then exchange with a partner who knows little about your topic. After your partner reads your description, ask her or him to summarize what you've explained so that you can tell if they understood it. If they do, you may have just discovered a skill you didn't know you have. If they don't, how would you rewrite your explanation to make it clearer?

Legal Eagles

As a class, brainstorm and then vote on an environmental issue that you care about. Is it protecting a local tree or animal? Is it cleaning up a local lake or river? Write a letter to your state senator and explain why this environmental issue is important to your class, community, and state. Ask your senator to sponsor a bill about your concern. If your senator agrees, your idea could become a bill and maybe even a law. Remember, government is of, by, and for the people—including you.

Campaign for Earth

Develop a campaign that encourages people to preserve and appreciate parts of your community—parks, woodlands, waterways, or wetlands. You could write a jingle, create a roadside billboard, or design a bumper sticker. If possible, present your campaign at a school assembly.

TOMMY HAYES
Charlestown High School

Next Stop, Nature

When you think about exploring nature, do you imagine busy streets and soaring skyscrapers? You would if you were in Tommy Hayes's class. Tommy and his students study the ecology of cities—how plants and animals live in environments built by people. Sometimes Tommy's classroom *is* Boston, like the time they investigated how noise pollution—from cars, buses, taxis, trucks, and construction—might affect birds.

City Song

Did you know that most birds communicate through song? When attracting a mate, they serenade in long, complex songs. When defending their territory, they usually warble shorter, simpler songs. Tommy's class hit the streets and digitally recorded the songs and locations of each bird they spotted—species like gold finches and song sparrows. Then they analyzed the loudness and pitch of the songs using special computer software. A year later, the class repeated the investigation. What did their study show? "Birds seemed to change their song pitch to be heard. They also seemed to be leaving the noisiest areas," says Tommy. Maybe the birds flew off to find a quiet place to sing without competition from car horns.

It's a Hit

When Tommy was young, he wanted to be a baseball player. But when he started working at a summer camp as a counselor, he changed his mind—becoming a teacher would be a real home run.

"I get to teach amazing, hardworking students from all backgrounds," says Tommy.

An environmental science teacher helps students learn about Earth's air, water, land, and life, and how they're all connected. Other **environmental science teachers** and their students

✳ participate in events such as cleaning up local environments.

✳ plant trees and investigate how they absorb CO_2 from the atmosphere.

✳ test the water quality of local streams.

Is It 4 U?

What parts of being a science teacher would you like?

- Coming up with cool investigations
- Taking students on field trips
- Exploring the ecology of your community
- Teaching students how to keep our planet healthy

Choose one of these and write a paragraph about how it can help students to enjoy science.

Helping Hand

Many scientists were inspired by a teacher. Make a thank-you card for a teacher who taught you something you'll never forget. Explain why you're grateful.

Feeder Reader

Whether your school is in the city, suburbs, or country, you and your classmates can collect data on birds in your area. It's simple. Put up a bird feeder. Then record the time of day and the kinds of birds who feed there.

To the Head of the Class

It's your turn to teach. Plan a 5-minute lesson about your local environment for classmates. Research an ecosystem near where you live—a forest, desert, seashore, or prairie. Create a detailed science illustration that shows the living creatures and the nonliving parts of the environment in which they live. Be sure to label your drawing. Include a caption that explains some of the ways the living things interact with each other and their surroundings. End your lesson with reasons why this ecosystem is important to your community.

WESLYNNE ASHTON

Yale School of Forestry and Environmental Studies

"I grew up surrounded by water, on an island in the Caribbean. I always thought I'd end up working with water."

While visiting a factory in Puerto Rico, Weslynne takes a minute to point out some of the natural beauty nearby.

Nature Nurtures

Flowers produce sweet nectar that bees rely on for food. And flowers rely on the bees to pollinate them while flying from blossom to blossom. It's a natural give-and-take—with nothing wasted. What if industrial parks worked the same way? Could businesses there cooperate in more natural ways too? Weslynne Ashton thinks so! "Nature has lots to teach us about how to survive—and thrive—by working together," Weslynne says.

Corporation Cooperation

Weslynne is an industrial ecologist. "That means I study clusters of industries that behave like ecosystems," she says. When they do, they help themselves—and the environment. In a dry area of Puerto Rico, Weslynne studied a cluster of factories that joined together to save water. First, a sewage plant cleans up wastewater. Next, a power plant turns that clean water into steam and produces electricity. A nearby refinery then uses that steam to turn oil into gasoline and other products. When the steam condenses back into water, it goes back to the power plant—and the cycle starts again. The give-and-take decreases waste and increases profits, Weslynne says. That's a real win-win!

An industrial ecologist

uses a combination of the environment, the economy and new technology to help businesses operate in a more sustainable way. Weslynne helps businesses incorporate the principles of natural systems to save money and energy. Other **industrial ecologists**

✸ design products that create less waste.

✸ help governments plan how they will reuse and recycle their resources.

✸ study the life cycle of products and businesses.

Close the Loop

Weslynne helps industries work together. How might the industries below cooperate to decrease waste, increase profits, and protect the environment?

• Fruit and vegetable farm
• Compost company
• Frozen fruit and vegetable packager

Draw a diagram that shows the order in which they could rely on one another. Then write a paragraph that explains your diagram.

Green Patrol

Talk to your teacher about setting up a class Green Patrol. Teams can have different "beats" such as

• posting "Please Don't Waste Water" signs.
• making sure lights, computers, and power strips are off at the end of the day.
• monitoring recycling bins to make sure they aren't being used for trash.
• turning off faucets so water doesn't leak.

I Am . . .

Weslynne's job often involves bringing businesses and people together to solve problems. Weslynne brings many skills to her job. She is *creative, inventive, friendly, organized, determined, cooperative,* and *a good communicator.* Make a list of the skills you have in common with Weslynne. What others can you include? Write down an example of how you use these skills in or out of school.

SYLVIA EARLE

Explorer in Residence
National Geographic

Water Woman

Sylvia Earle remembers the moment the sea swept her off her feet—literally and figuratively. When that wave hit, "it was pretty exciting," she says. "But what really captured my attention as a kid and still does, and always will, is the enormous diversity of life in the ocean."

The Sturgeon General

"The ocean governs the way this planet works," Sylvia says. And if we could pick someone to govern the sea, we'd pick Sylvia—"Her Deepness," as many call her. She's swum with singing whales, advised presidents on policy, and walked on the seafloor deeper than any other human. Sylvia's spent her career exploring our delicate biosphere—"our life support system," as she calls it—and trying to protect it. She even started a submarine company, to help us get a better look at its deepest, wettest parts.

Swayed by the Sea

When asked if she wants to be known as a scientist, author, environmentalist, explorer, educator, or entrepreneur, Sylvia replies, "All of the above. And as somebody who cares." For example, Sylvia no longer eats seafood. "I know too many fish personally," she laughs.

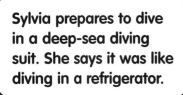

Sylvia prepares to dive in a deep-sea diving suit. She says it was like diving in a refrigerator.

An oceanographer studies the plants, animals, and microbes that live in ocean ecosystems. Sylvia dives and documents life undersea, and shares her research through books, lectures, and films. Other **oceanographers**

✳ protect coral reefs from destruction.

✳ track whales from Alaska to Hawaii.

✳ work at aquariums.

✳ investigate deep-ocean currents.

The Oceans and U

We share Earth with countless ocean creatures—from microscopic plankton to massive whales. Write a paragraph that begins with the following topic sentence. *Ocean creatures depend on us—just as we depend on them—to keep our planet healthy*. Then write an explanation that tells what it means. Your explanation should

- include one or two reasons that support the topic sentence.
- include a few examples that support your reasons.
- end by summarizing what you've said and explaining why it's important.

Oceans 5

With a partner, take an ocean voyage around the world. Using a map, start with any ocean and see if you can trace your finger from that ocean back to where you started. Stay on an ocean the whole time. Draw a flowchart of your route around the world and the order of the oceans that you passed through. Below your flowchart, write your answers to these questions. Be sure to use complete sentences.

- What did you learn about the oceans?
- In which ocean would you like to deep-sea dive to learn more?
- What sea life might you see during your dive?

About You

As a girl, Sylvia loved playing with horseshoe crabs on the beach, even though adults told her they were dangerous. "That gave me self-confidence about trusting my own observations. And that's one of the first marks of being a scientist." What makes you a good scientist?

"Ecologists know that nature is really very complex."

RODOLFO DIRZO
Stanford University

Disappearing Act

"Many things in nature seem mysterious at first," tropical ecologist Rodolfo Dirzo says. "But they make sense if you look at how they are all connected." For example, what happens when big animals, like Mexican jaguars, start disappearing? The animals that jaguars hunt become too plentiful. Then the plants those animals eat start disappearing. Nature is thrown out of balance. That delicate balance intrigues Rodolfo. Rodolfo's research focuses on what happens when humans cut down rain forests, specifically in his native Mexico. If the remaining patches of rain forest become too small or too far apart, animals, such as jaguars, might not be able to survive there.

Clever Clover

Not only do plants and animals depend on each other, explains Rodolfo, but they can also actually change in response to each other. In college, Rodolfo studied clover that isn't poisonous except when it grows near slugs that might eat it. Stay away! Exploring nature has always fascinated him. As a young boy in Mexico, Rodolfo liked to catch butterflies and explore forests and canyons. That passion inspired him to become the first in his family to go to college. There, Rodolfo's studies inspired him to keep investigating his world.

Rodolfo measures the diameter of a tree in Los Tuxtlas tropical forest in Veracruz, Mexico.

A tropical ecologist studies the ways forest communities of plants and animals live. They also study things that might affect the forest's health, such as logging. Rodolfo studies how plants and animals adapt, especially in tropical rain forests. Other **tropical ecologists**

✳ study how non-native plants and animals affect natural balances.

✳ try to determine why certain plants or animals are disappearing.

✳ help create laws and policies that protect the environment.

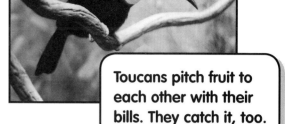

Toucans pitch fruit to each other with their bills. They catch it, too.

About You

Rodolfo was inspired by *On the Origin of Species*, a book by Charles Darwin. What books have inspired you?

Corridor Connection

Buildings, roads, and crop fields often break up ecosystems. That's why people are setting aside wildlife corridors. Corridors provide a way for animals and plants to move from one isolated patch of an ecosystem to another. If food is scarce in one patch, animals can use the corridor to reach another patch. With a team, brainstorm an area in your community where you could create a wildlife corridor. Draw a map that shows its location and how you could connect two patches of an ecosystem. What kinds of wildlife could your corridor help? How?

Eco-Travel

As a class, create a brochure that will help tourists safely and respectfully enjoy a rain forest. Select a rain forest somewhere in the world. Divide into teams to work on the following.

• A description of the rain forest
• Fun facts about its unique ecology
• A science illustration of one plant and one animal
• A list of reasons why the rain forest should be protected
• A map of the country that shows where the rain forest is located
• A list of fun activities to do such as hike; use a field guide to identify plants, animals, insects, and birds; ride a zip line across the canopy; and photograph wildlife

Then, put your brochure together.

SUSAN MURCOTT
Massachusetts Institute of Technology

Hauling H$_2$O

For most of us, clean water is as easy to get as turning on a faucet. But for nearly one billion people around the world, getting water for cooking, drinking, and bathing isn't nearly that easy. It can mean hauling heavy buckets from a faraway well or river. Even worse, chemical runoff, waste, or microorganisms might contaminate the water. That's where Susan Murcott comes in.

Clean-up Act

With her student teams, Susan develops innovative ways to filter contaminants from drinking water. She works in some of the world's poorest places—from Burma to Nicaragua—to develop water treatment systems that fit local needs. For people living in remote areas of Nepal, that meant creating a filter to remove poisonous arsenic from well water. "Our partners have included university-educated people as well as uneducated villagers. We work together on a common need—safe, clean drinking water for all."

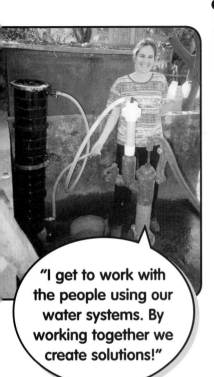

"I get to work with the people using our water systems. By working together we create solutions!"

Thirsty for More

Susan didn't study much science when she was younger. After college, she was a writer, but she was thirsty for more. "I really wanted practical skills, like engineering," she says. So, Susan went back to school and studied environmental engineering. Now she brings safe water to millions.

"Water treatment is *really* needed in the developing world—where I want to continue to work."

A water engineer designs and builds systems that purify and bring water to people. Susan makes filters and helps people all over the world gain access to safe, clean water. Other **water engineers**

✳ create water conservation technology.

✳ build systems that dispose of wastewater and sewage.

✳ design ways to prevent floods from damaging towns and cities.

✳ invent new methods for preparing for droughts.

The Yangtze River is the third longest river in the world.

What Do You Think?

Water is Earth's most precious resource. Do you agree with this statement? If so, write a persuasive essay about why you agree. If you disagree, write a persuasive essay about what natural resource you think is more precious. Be sure to

• begin your essay with a statement about your position.

• state two or three reasons that support your position.

• write a separate paragraph for each of your supporting reasons that will persuade your reader.

• write a concluding paragraph that summarizes your position.

Go with the Flow

Mountain glaciers fill many major rivers around the world. Team up with a partner. Trace the following rivers on a world map and name the country or countries each flows through— Ganges, Indus, Mekong, and Yangtze rivers. Then create a map that traces one of these rivers from where it starts to where it ends. Show and label the countries through which the rivers run.

Are U in Shape?

Many people around the world must haul water from a river or well to their home every day. Imagine carrying drinking water to your class every day. Water weighs about 1 kilogram (2.2 pounds) per liter—water molecules are small but heavy. Each one of your classmates needs about 1.9 liters—eight 8-ounce glasses—of drinking water each day. How many kilograms of water would you have to carry each day?

Check out your answers on page 36.

WINDI PADIA

Colorado Division of Wildlife

Dial 911 for Wildlife

You walk out of the mall and there in the parking lot is . . . a big black bear! Now what? This is a job for Windi Padia, wildlife officer—a sort of police officer for the wilderness. She protects wildlife, including wild plants and animals, and natural resources, such as rivers and streams. "A wildlife officer is a lot of different things," Windi explains. "But I'd say I'm an advocate for wildlife . . . they don't have a voice."

Call of the Wild

After studying ecology and evolutionary biology at Princeton University, Windi took a sales job at a pharmaceutical company, but her heart wasn't in it. So she hung up her business suits and returned to Colorado to become a wildlife officer. "I was always happiest when I was outdoors near wildlife," Windi says.

Wilderness Work

Some days, Windi patrols the wilderness by truck or on horseback, enforcing fishing and hunting laws. Other days, she teaches children about ecosystems or helps farmers deal with damage caused by wildlife. And, yes, she responds to calls about wild animals on the loose. Windi once removed a sleeping 125-pound bear from a tree near downtown Boulder!

After tranquilizing it, Windi and her co-workers returned this tree-rific member of the bear species to the wilderness.

Windi is **a wildlife officer** who patrols an area of Colorado and helps keep the peace between humans and animals. **Wildlife officers** also

* assist biologists in studying migration patterns and tracking animal populations.

* educate the public about animal behavior.

* develop conservation programs to protect endangered plants and animals.

Fitness Works

Being physically fit is important to Windi's job. She danced ballet for 13 years and has a black belt in martial arts. What do you do to keep your body healthy?

What Am I?

The image above shows the only flying mammal. What is it? While some species of this mammal number in the millions, many species are endangered.

The Name Game

Wildlife officers can identify animals from a distance. How? By their size, shape, and unique features. Windi sent these drawings of three members of the deer family that live in Colorado. In small groups, discuss what features you think helps Windi identify them. Can you identify them? Draw your own profiles of members of an animal from the same family, such as Felidae—cats! Exchange with other teams and see if you can identify their unique features.

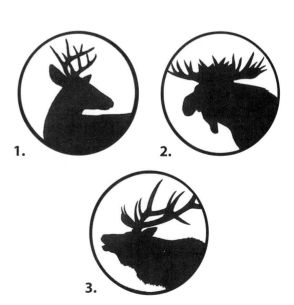

1.

2.

3.

Check out your answers on page 36.

About Me

The more you know about yourself, the better you'll be able to plan your future. Start an **About Me Journal** to help you investigate your interests, and scout out your skills and strengths.

Record the date in your journal. Then copy each of the 15 statements below, and write down your responses. Revisit your journal a few times a year to find out how you've changed and grown.

1. *These are things I'd like to do someday.*
   Choose from this list, or create your own.

   - Design new ways to use energy
   - Develop a conservation project
   - Conduct experiments in space
   - Study the effects of climate change
   - Invent ways to distribute clean water
   - Walk on the seafloor
   - Produce movies
   - Explore the ecology of cities
   - Teach science
   - Help clean up the environment
   - Design eco-friendly products

2. *These would be part of the perfect job.*
   Choose from this list, or create your own.

   - Being outdoors
   - Making things
   - Writing
   - Designing a project
   - Observing
   - Being indoors
   - Drawing
   - Investigating
   - Leading others
   - Communicating

3. *These are things that interest me.*
   Here are some of the interests that people in this book had when they were young. They might inspire some ideas for your journal.

- Learning to fly an airplane
- Exploring swamps, forests, or canyons
- Examining rocks and plants
- Doing cool science experiments
- Working as a camp counselor

- Swimming in the ocean
- Catching butterflies
- Ice skating
- Walking on the beach
- Playing baseball
- Going to college

4. *These are my favorite subjects in school.*

5. *These are my favorite places to go on field trips.*

6. *These are things I like to investigate in my free time.*

7. *When I work on teams, I like to do this kind of work.*

8. *When I work alone, I like to do this kind of work.*

9. *These are my strengths—in and out of school.*

10. *These things are important to me—in and out of school.*

11. *These are three activities I like to do.*

12. *These are three activities I don't like to do.*

13. *These are three people I admire.*

14. *If I could invite a special guest to school for the day, this is who I'd choose, and why.*

15. *This is my dream career.*

Environmental Sciences

Which ^career is 4 U?

What do you need to do to get there? Do some research and ask some questions. Then, take your ideas about your future—plus inspiration from scientists you've read about—and have a blast mapping out your goals.

On paper or poster board, map your plan. Draw three columns labeled **Middle School**, **High School**, and **College**. Then draw three rows labeled **Classes**, **Electives**, and **Other Activities**. Now, fill in your future.

Don't hold back—reach for the stars!

Air Quality Engineer

Microbial Ecologist

Environmental Film Producer

Natural Resource Manager

Climate Change Biologist

Hydrologist

Atmospheric Chemist

Ecologist

Oceanographer

Developmental
Biologist

Chemist

Tropical
Ecologist

Astronaut

Science
Teacher

Marine Biologist

Renewable
Energy Engineer

Wildlife
Officer

Geochemist

Botanist

Industrial
Ecologist

Environmental
Reporter

Conservation
Scientist

Water
Engineer

Science
Illustrator

Agroecologist

Meteorologist

amphibian (n.) A class of cold-blooded vertebrates, including toads, frogs, newts, and salamanders. Amphibians live partly in water and partly on land. They have four legs and a moist smooth skin without scales. They lay eggs that are not protected by a shell. (pp. 10, 11)

biofuel (n.) A fuel made from renewable resources such as plants or municipal wastes that replaces or reduces the use of fossil fuels such as gasoline. (p. 13)

biology (n.) The study of living things. It includes the study of how plants, animals, and microorganisms develop, live, reproduce, and interact with their environment. (pp. 8, 9, 10, 11, 29, biologist p.28)

biosphere (n.) The relatively narrow region of air, water, and land on Earth's surface that supports life. The biosphere is made up of different biomes. (p. 22)

botany (n.) The branch of biology that deals with the study of plants. It includes many areas such as plant structure, function, geographical distribution, and classification. (p. 6)

conservation (n.) The protection of the natural world from the effects of human activities. This includes the protection of endangered species and valuable natural environments, such as the rain forests and coral reefs. It also includes protection from pollution, and recycling of water, glass, paper, plastics, and some metals. (pp. 27, 29, 30)

contaminate (v.) To make something impure by adding, or exposing it to, a poisonous or polluting substance. (p. 26)

drought (n.) An extended period of unusually low rainfall, resulting in a shortage of water. (p. 27)

ecology (n.) The study of the relationships between living organisms and the nonliving environment in which they live. (pp. 18, 19, 28, 30, ecologist pp. 20, 21)

ecosystem (n.) All of the living organisms (plant, animal, and microscopic species) in a given area that interact with each other and their surrounding environment. (pp. 9, 19, 20, 23, 25, 28)

endangered species (n.) A species at the brink of extinction. (p. 29)

engineering (n.) The application of science and mathematics to design and build structures, such as bridges and wind turbines, and products, such as cell phones and biofuels. (pp. 14, 26)

food chain (n.) A series of living organisms in an ecosystem that are linked by the order of who eats whom. (p. 7)

gene (n.) The unit of heredity in living organisms that determines the characteristics that an offspring inherits from its parent or parents. (p. 11)

geologist (n.) A person who studies the science of rocks to learn about the history and structure of Earth. (p. 9)

geothermal (adj.) Natural steam produced deep inside Earth that can be used to generate electricity. (p. 13)

microorganism (n.) (also known as a microbe) A form of life, usually single-celled, that is too small to be seen without a microscope—including bacteria, some fungi, and some protists. (pp. 23, 26)

migration (n.) The seasonal movement of certain animals, mostly birds and fish, to distant places for breeding or feeding. (p. 29)

technology (n.) The application of scientific knowledge for practical purposes. (pp. 21, 27)

Index

amphibian, 10, 11
animals, 8, 9, 23, 24, 25, 29
aquariums, 23
Arctic sea ice, 9
astronaut, 6, 7

biologist, 11, 29
biosphere, 22
birds, 18, 19
botany, 6

California coast, 16, 17
carbon dioxide, 6, 9
Charlestown High School, 18
chemical runoff, 26
clean drinking water, 26, 27
climate change, 8, 16
climate change biologist, 8, 9
Colorado Division of Wildlife, 28
compost, 21
computer software, 18
conservation programs, 29
coral reefs, 9, 14, 15, 23

Darwin, Charles, 25
deep-sea diving, 22, 23
deep-sea ocean currents, 23
desert, 11, 19
developmental biologist, 10, 11
documentaries, 15
droughts, 27

Earth, 6, 7, 23
Earth's warming, effects of, 9
ecologist, 16, 24
ecology, 18, 19, 25, 28
ecosystem, 9, 11, 19, 20, 25, 28
Edith's checkerspot butterfly, 8, 9
electricity, 12, 13, 20
endangered, 15, 17, 29
  animals, 29
  plants, 29
  species, 17, 29
  wildlife, 15
energy, 7, 12, 13, 21
energy engineer, 12, 13

engineers, 6, 12
environment, 14, 15, 18, 19, 20
environment, protection of, 17, 21, 25
environmental, 6, 10, 13, 15, 16, 17, 26
  disasters, 15
  engineer, 6
  engineering, 26
  impact, 13
  issue, 17
  legislation, 17
  pollutants, 10
  scientists, 16
  studies, 17
environmental film producer, 14, 15
environmentalist, 6, 14, 22
environmental lawyer, 16, 17
environmental science teacher, 18, 19
evolutionary biology, 28
Explorer in Residence, National Geographic, 22

field guide, 9
field journal, 9
field trips, 19
fieldwork, 9, 11
film production, 15
films, 14, 23
filter, 26, 27
fishing laws, 28
flood prevention, 27
food chain, 7
forest, 9, 11, 19, 24, 25
frogs, 10, 11

Ganges, 27
genes, 11
geologist, 9
glaciers, 27
global warming, 6, 15
Going Green Action Plan, 13
gravity, 7

habitats, 8, 9
hunting laws, 28

IMAX movies, 14, 15
Indus, 27
industrial ecologist, 20, 21
industries, 20, 21

lawsuits, 17
life cycle, 11, 21

Magellan spacecraft, 6
mammals, 11
marine life, 16
Massachusetts Institute of Technology, 26
mechanical energy, 12
Mekong, 27
microbes, 23
microorganisms, 26
microscopic plankton, 23
migration patterns, 29
movies, 14, 15

NASA, 6
natural fires, 15
natural resources, 27, 28
natural systems, 21
noise pollution, 18

observation, 9, 23
ocean, 6, 7, 9, 14, 22, 23
  ecosystems, 23
  engineering, 14
  temperatures, 7, 9
oceanographer, 22, 23
oil, 15, 16, 20
  drilling, 16
  spills, 15
On the Origin of Species, 25
organisms, 9, 11

photosynthesis, 7
phytoplankton, 6, 7
plant life, 6, 7
plants, 8, 9, 23, 24, 25, 28
  nonnative, 25
pollution, 17
power grid, 13
power plant, 20
producer, 14, 15

rain forests, 14, 24, 25
recycling, 13, 15, 17, 21
renewable energy, 12
research, 8, 11, 19, 23
resources, 21
rivers, 27, 28

satellites, 6, 7
  data, 6
  images, 7
science illustration, 19, 25

scientific experiments, 6, 7
sea water analysis, 16
sewage disposal, 27
sewage plant, 20
Shuttle missions, 7
Sigma Space Corporation, 6
single cell, 11
Space Shuttle, 6
species, 8, 11
steam condensation, 20
stem cells, 11

tide pools, 16
tropical ecologist, 24, 25
tropical rain forest, 24, 25

undersea life, 23
University, 8, 10, 12, 14, 16, 24, 28
  American University, 14
  Princeton University, 28
  Stanford University, 16, 24
  University of California, Berkeley, 10
  University of Texas at Austin, 8, 12

wastewater, 20, 27
water, 11, 19, 26, 27
  conservation technology, 27
  pollution, 11
  quality, 19
  treatment systems, 26
water engineer, 26, 27
wetland, 11, 17
whales, 14, 16, 23
wildlife, 14, 15, 17, 25, 28
  advocate, 28
  corridors, 25
  organizations, 15
  protection, 15, 28
wildlife officer, 28, 29
wind, 12, 13
wind turbines, 12, 13

Yale School of Forestry and Environmental Studies, 20
Yangtze, 27

CHECK OUT YOUR ANSWERS

ASTRONAUT, page 7

Phyto Flight

DEVELOPMENTAL BIOLOGIST, page 11

Frog versus Toad

Frogs	Overlap	Toads
• Live in moist environments • Have smooth or slimy skin • Have long, webbed hind feet for jumping and swimming • Lay eggs in clusters	• Both are amphibians. • Both are herbivores as tadpoles, carnivores as adults. • Both have metamorphic life cycles—eggs, then tadpoles, then adults.	• Live in dry environments • Have warty, leathery skin • Have short hind legs for walking • Lay eggs in long chains

ENERGY ENGINEER, page 13

On the Rise

Circle graph for 2007—8.4 percent renewable energies, 91.6 percent nonrewable energies; circle graph for 2030—12.5 percent renewable energy, 87.5 percent nonrenewable energy. It's important to increase our use of renewable energy so that we depend less on fossil fuels. Fossil fuels release gases such as carbon dioxide into the air. Some, such as carbon dioxide, are changing Earth's climate. Others are harmful to people. Switching to cleaner energy sources can help create a more Earth-friendly future.

Blowing in the Wind

$$32.8 \text{ households} = 350,000 \text{ kilowatt hours electricity} \times \frac{1 \text{ household}}{10,655 \text{ kilowatt hours electricity}}$$

WATER ENGINEER, page 27

Are U in Shape?

$$28 \text{ students} \times 1.9 \text{ liters} \times \frac{1 \text{ kilogram}}{1 \text{ liter}} = 53.2 \text{ kilograms}$$

WILDLIFE OFFICER, page 29

What Am I?

a bat

The Name Game

1. Mule Deer
2. Moose
3. Elk

IMAGE CREDITS

Mike Dunn, NC Museum of Natural Sciences: Cover. Jim Zuckerman/Corbis: pp. 2-5 and pp. 30-31 background. © NASA/Renee Bouchard: p. 2 (Cleave), p. 6 top. Erin McCarley: p. 2 (Santoso), p. 12. American University: p. 2 (Palmer). Cristina Cabrera-Barros: p. 3 (Ashton), p. 20 bottom. NREL: p. 3 (Dirzo). © Rebecca Lawson Photography: p. 4. NASA: p. 5, p. 6 bottom, p. 7, p. 33 top right. Stuart Westmorland/Corbis: pp. 6-29 banner. Jeffrey S. Pippen: p. 9. Kris Holland: p. 11. Lori Haven, Teacher, R.F. Kennedy School, San Jose: p. 13. Sara Wipfler: p. 14 top. Nic Coury: p. 16 top. © Andrew Howe: p. 19. Elizabeth Cole: p. 20 top. EPA: p. 21. NOAA: p. 22 bottom, p.33 top left. Kristian Sekulic: p. 23. Tom Kelly: p. 26. The Daily Camera: p. 28 bottom. Colorado Division of Wildlife: p. 29 bottom. Clara Lam: p. 30. Scott Bauer/USDA: p. 32 left, p. 33 bottom left, p. 33 bottom right. Planetary Coral Reef Foundation/Michel Lippitsch: p. 32 right.